I0815384

Monster Jokes

Joe King

Abdo Kids Junior
is an Imprint of Abdo Kids
abdobooks.com

Abdo
ABDO KIDS JOKES
Kids

abdobooks.com

Published by Abdo Kids, a division of ABDO, P.O. Box 398166, Minneapolis, Minnesota 55439.

Printed in China

052023

092023

Photo Credits: Getty Images, Shutterstock

Production Contributors: Teddy Borth, Jennie Forsberg, Grace Hansen

Design Contributors: Candice Keimig, Pakou Moua

Library of Congress Control Number: 2022946712

Publisher's Cataloging-in-Publication Data

Names: King, Joe, author.

Title: Monster jokes / by Joe King

Description: Minneapolis, Minnesota : Abdo Kids, 2024 | Series: Abdo kids jokes | Includes online resources and index.

Identifiers: ISBN 9781098266073 (lib. bdg.) | ISBN 9781098266776 (ebook) | ISBN 9781098267124 (Read-to-me ebook)

Subjects: LCSH: Jokes--Juvenile literature. | Wit and humor--Juvenile literature. | Monsters--Juvenile literature. | Humor--Juvenile literature.

Classification: DDC 818.6--dc23

Table of Contents

Monster Jokes

What's a vampire's favorite fruit?

Necktarines!

How can you tell that a vampire has a cold?

He starts coffin.

What do you get when you cross a vampire and a snowman?
Frostbite!

What do witches like to eat at the beach?

Sandwiches!

What happened to the witch who didn't follow the rules at school?

She was exspelled!

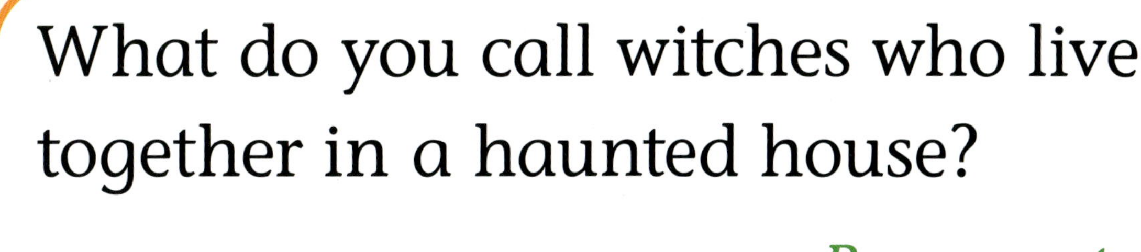

What do you call witches who live together in a haunted house?

Broommates.

Did you use all of my wart cream?!

What do mummies put on their bagels?

Scream cheese.

What ride do little mummies like best at the amusement park?

The scary-go-round!

What does the mummy do at the library?
He gets wrapped up in a good book!
Breaking Ancient Egyptian Curses for Dummies

What did the critics say about Frankenstein's art project?

It's a monsterpiece.

How does Frankenstein's Monster leave the party?

He bolts!

Who did Frankenstein's
Monster take to the dance?
His ghoul friend.
I hope they play
scary styles!

What position did the zombie play on the soccer team?

Ghoulie.

Why couldn't the zombie go to school at Hogwarts?

He couldn't spell.

What did the zombies say to the villagers?
Pleased to eat you!
eeek!
This street is a dead end!

How does a ghost sneeze?

Ahh...ahh...ahh...BOO!

Why did the ghost blow its nose?

Because it was full of booo-gers!

What do ghosts eat for dinner?
Spook-etti.
Trick or eat!

What did the werewolf ask his friend?

Howl's it going?

What do you call a monster that says bad words?

A swearwolf.

What did the werewolf say to his dinner guests?
Bone-appetit!
HOWL-ARIOUS!

How did Poseidon greet the sea monster?

Hey buddy, what's kraken?

What type of monster loves dance music?

The boogie man.

What is a sea monster's favorite snack?
Ships and dip.
I need 8 napkins!

How does a monster start a bedtime story?

Once upon a slime…

What birthday cake do monsters like best?

Ice-scream cake.

What is a dangerous way to reach the attic of a haunted house?

The monstairs.

- Know your audience
- Timing is everything
- Confidence is key
- Go out on a high note!

Glossary

bon appétit
French for "good appetite" but meaning "enjoy your meal."

critic
a person whose work is to judge and write opinions about movies and other art forms.

pun
a joke using a word that sounds like a different word or has another meaning. Examples from this book are "slime" (time) and "ships and dip" (chips and dip).

Index